Foreign Affairs
A New Financial Geopolitics?

Foreign Affairs January 2018

The U.S.-Led Monetary Order in
a Time of Turbulence

TABLE OF CONTENTS

Introduction

Mark Blyth and Sylvia Maxfield

After the election of Donald Trump to the presidency, there were wide expectations that the market would respond negatively to his unexpected victory. And yet stock markets rose globally and remain up today. Bond markets have not unwound as predicted, and overall, business as usual seems to be the order of the day in global finance. In an age of political turbulence, the financial world, at least, seems rather stable.

Perhaps this is not so surprising. After all, during the 2008 financial crisis, though the turmoil originated in the United States, the U.S. dollar went up, not down, and the euro proved itself to be a less-than-perfect substitute as a number of debt crises rattled the European continent. And although China managed to maneuver the renminbi into the International Monetary Fund's Special Drawing Rights basket (a synthetic reserve that also includes the U.S. dollar, British pound sterling, Japanese yen, and euro), it's still not an internationalized currency. Lacking substitutes, the dollar-driven order rumbles on.

This special Foreign Affairs' anthology examines whether, despite this surface calm, the geopolitics of finance has shifted over the last decade, given the near collapse of the world's banking systems and the rise of populists and nationalists all eager to change the status quo in one way or another. What might be the fault lines in the financial world that could precipitate another crisis, and possible realignments, in the global monetary order?

Our first two contributions from Jacqueline Best and Sandy Hager highlight risks within the U.S.-led order itself. Best explores the much-trumpeted independence of central banks, which is what makes them so effective in managing financial crises and yet renders them so unpopular in a world awash with populist fervor. Hager, meanwhile, looks at whether there could be alternatives to a dollar-led order. The second two pieces take us across the Atlantic to assess the state of the European financial order. Kathleen McNamara warns of the remarkable fragility of Europe's system. Simon Tilford and Mark Blyth argue, in turn, how fundamental imbalances within the eurozone may split it into two distinct segments over the long term. Finally, Saori Katada and Hongying Wang look at Asian alternatives to the dollar-led order. Katada reminds us of the attempt in the 1990s to make the yen an international rival to the dollar, and highlights the lessons learned from that episode. Wang, meanwhile, discusses China's reluctance to internationalize its currency.

In sum, the contributors to this special issue have sought to identify the potential weaknesses of our current financial system and whether or not there are alternatives to replace it. For now, it would likely take a particularly unlikely concatenation of negative shocks to seriously challenge the dollar-led order. But then again, so was the 2008 financial crisis, the vote for Brexit, the rise of Trump, and the ability of so many populist movements to muscle their way into power in Europe. Although our analysis suggests more stability than the volatility of the daily news flow would suggest, we should not forget the "tail risk" that such systems generate. Indeed, it's often in moments where we are most sure things are solid that they sometimes "melt into air."

MARK BLYTH is Eastman Professor of Political Economy at Brown University. SYLVIA MAXFIELD is Dean of the Providence College School of Business.

Bring Politics Back to Monetary Policy

How Technocratic Exceptionalism Fuels Populism

Jacqueline Best

Federal Reserve Chair Janet Yellen testifies at the Senate Banking, Housing, and Urban Affairs Committee, February 2014.

The current battle over the liberal world order seems to be about trade, climate, and security policy. But monetary policy has also become an increasingly important arena of conflict. Populist leaders seem to love nothing more than denouncing central bankers and challenging the legitimacy of the current monetary order, as Donald Trump famously did during the U.S. presidential election campaign when he accused central bankers of "doing political things" by keeping interest rates low.

In responding to this challenge, it is tempting to point to central banks' independence from politics as a defense against the dangers posed by erratic leaders. Yet that would be a risky move. It turns out that decades of appeals to technocratic exceptionalism—the idea that monetary policy should be shielded from democratic oversight—have had costs. Indeed, this exceptionalism can lead to the very politicization of monetary policy that it seeks to avoid.

Central banks play a paradoxical role in today's liberal democracies. Their work is highly technical, yet the consequences of their actions are inevitably political, producing big winners and losers. They wield great power in democratic societies, and yet they are unelected—because of the fear that politicians tend to push up inflation to appease their bases unless interest rate policy is insulated from democratic pressures.

The underlying tensions in central banks' technocratic exceptionalism became particularly evident in the aftermath of the 2008 global financial crisis. In recent years, the banks' entire mission has become unclear: for decades, they have been focused on fighting inflation, yet since the crisis there has been no inflation to worry about despite massive central bank interventions. In fact, the opposite fear—this time, of deflation—has driven extraordinarily loose policies and a great deal of experimentation, ranging from massive bailouts to quantitative easing and ultra-low (even negative) interest rates. Although more normal conditions appear to be on the way at last, the decade of exceptional policies has taken its toll on the legitimacy of the current global monetary order.

The loudest critics of central banks have been on the populist right: Victor Orban's regime in Hungary, pro-Brexit forces in the United Kingdom, Marine Le Pen's Front National in France, Tea Party Republicans, and even President Donald Trump in the United States. Riding the growing wave of public skepticism about experts and elites, these illiberal populists have identified central bankers as among the worst offenders.

A decade of exceptional policies has taken its toll on the legitimacy of the current global monetary order.

To save the current monetary architecture from such challenges—an absolutely vital task in a world in which the reliable circulation of money serves as the foundation for economic and political stability—monetary policy needs to have a more robust form of democratic accountability built in. Only then can nations ensure that central banks genuinely meet the needs of those for whom they work: the people.

Of course, with the forces of populist illiberalism on the rise, it is hard not to be relieved that at least some aspects of economic policy are insulated from political oversight. If central bank independence is supposed to protect monetary policy from excessive political pressure, then what better example of its merits than the fact that at least a little of the economy is off-limits to the Orbans and Trumps of the world?

Yet there is a peculiar irony at work here: this argument suggests that our best response to illiberal tendencies is an equally illiberal strategy of excluding monetary policies from democratic accountability. Although technocratic exceptionalism is tempting, especially in the face of the threat of illiberal democracy, it is also quite dangerous, since it reduces accountability even as it never quite succeeds in getting the politics out of monetary policy. This disconnect with the public ultimately fuels the kind of populist backlash the world has recently seen, further politicizing monetary policy with potentially very worrying consequences.

People wait for a Janet Yellen press conference in Washington, D.C., June 2017.

LIBERAL EXCEPTIONALISM

The word "exceptionalist" is typically used to describe an American sense of uniqueness and exemption from the usual global rules. But in this article, I draw instead on an analysis of liberal exceptionalism that focuses on security policy: situations in which political leaders invoke a state of exception to justify the suspension of liberal democratic rights in order to respond to a severe threat to the nation. This might seem an unlikely place to begin a reflection on contemporary economic policy, but there are rather obvious and important parallels.

This kind of exceptionalism dates back to the Roman practice of dictatorship, which allowed a republic to temporarily cede power to a military leader for a six-month period in order to fight a war. Modern liberal democracies have adopted their own strategies for responding rapidly to a variety of crises, including by building various exceptionalist provisions (such as states of emergency) into their legal systems. These enable the democracies to bypass slower deliberative processes in crisis situations.

Although such temporary states of exception have long existed in democratic societies, they have also, appropriately, been the subject of great debate, since they run the risk of eroding the very rights that they seek to protect. Not surprisingly, following 9/11 when many Western states suspended various liberal democratic rights in the name of a security emergency, there was a resurgence of interest in such debates. In that case, and in the case of most exceptionalist security strategies, there is a general pattern in which an initial declaration of an existential threat to the state (such as the attacks on the Twin Towers) justifies the temporary suspension of normal liberal democratic processes and rights (such as privacy rights), which is then institutionalized through a range of legal, extra-legal, and bureaucratic procedures (such as the use widespread civilian surveillance).

A great deal of ink has been spilled on security exceptionalism, but there has been very little attention paid to its place in economic policy. That is surprising, because the history of exceptionalist policy in the West is chock full of cases in which emergency provisions have been used to pursue economic ends. Witness the regular reliance on martial law in the nineteenth and early twentieth centuries to put down strikes deemed a threat to the nation in both the United States and the United Kingdom, or the use by U.S. President Franklin D. Roosevelt of the Trading with the Enemy Act of 1917 to stop a run on the banks by banning the private ownership of gold.

In both of these cases, we can see the familiar logic of exceptionalism: a declaration of a serious threat to the nation, the temporary suspension of normal liberal democratic rights, and the implementation of a range of policies designed to put that exception into place.

Although a free market economy often supports political stability, the recent global financial crisis reminds that it is also prone to regular and devastating crises.

ECONOMIC EXCEPTIONALISM IN TIMES OF CRISIS

Beyond the familiar tension between the liberal commitment to rights and the demands of security, exceptionalist politics attempt to resolve another tension at the heart of liberal democracy: the one between the goals of a stable democratic polity and those of a free market economy. Although a free market economy often supports political stability, the recent global financial crisis reminds that it is also prone to regular and devastating crises.

In such moments of crisis, political leaders have often declared a state of economic exception and have suspended normal liberal democratic norms and rights. For example, during the recent financial crisis, we saw a wide range of emergency economic measures pushed rapidly through legislative processes or introduced in quasi-legal fashion in order to halt the hemorrhaging of the global credit system. As in the case of security exceptions, political leaders generally argued that speed was of the essence and that the normal processes of democratic deliberation must therefore be bypassed.

Their decisions were nothing new. Writing after the Great Depression and the Second World War, the Austro-Hungarian economists Karl Polanyi and Friedrich Hayek both identified the double tension in liberalism, ultimately proposing radically different solutions. Polanyi argued in The Great Transformation that one of the major causes of the dislocations of the 1930s and 1940s was that an unchecked economy had ultimately produced great crises and profoundly reactionary responses. His answer to this core tension was to constrain the excesses of the market for the sake of democratic stability. In The Road to Serfdom, Hayek put forward a very different diagnosis, arguing that it was insufficient market freedom that had opened the door to the rise of fascism. He therefore argued for the opposite response, calling for market freedom to be protected at all costs.

If Polanyi's solution held sway throughout the Keynesian postwar years, Hayek has won the day since the rise of neoliberalism in the 1980s. His strategy and the profound skepticism about democracy that it embodies underpin the vast majority of today's dominant economic theories, as well as many of the economic practices that they justify. For example, public choice theories of rent-seeking and bureaucratic expansion urge mistrust of elected politicians and public servants and the avoidance of relying on the government to provide necessary services. Meanwhile, both the theory of political business cycles and the time-inconsistency hypothesis predict that politicians will tend to promise low inflation early in their terms but will ultimately pursue expansionary policies just before elections, creating dangerous inflationary pressures.

By telling us to be wary of too much democracy, and demarcating a range of different economic problems that must be protected from its influence, these policy practices effectively create and reproduce little pockets of exceptionalism on an everyday basis. Economic exceptionalism thus takes two rather different forms in contemporary liberal democratic states. When major crises hit, we often find governments using emergency exceptionalism to give them the power to pull out all the stops in response. At the same time, the underlying fear of too much political intervention has produced a second technocratic form of exceptionalism, which carves off certain areas of policy as too important to be subject to democratic whim. Paying attention to the role of these different kinds of economic exceptionalism tells us a great deal about how central banks worked up until the 2008 global financial crisis and how they have struggled to make things work since then.

THE HAYEKIAN REVOLUTION

Central bankers today see their job as fighting inflation, and they derive their legitimacy from doing so effectively. But with inflation rates at historic lows, and with the global economy in a very different state than it was several decades ago, the decision to continue to make inflation the principal (and in some cases the sole) focus of monetary policy should be seen as a political choice. It is important to ask whether the goal of fighting inflation, however noble that pursuit might be, justifies essentially undemocratic means.

The doctrine of central bank independence and the narrow focus on very low inflation are quite recent innovations, dating back to the same Hayekian revolution in political economic policy in the 1980s. Before then, policymakers took a more Polanyian approach, tailoring monetary policy to meet a range of political goals. With the pain of the Great Depression still in recent memory, policymakers put more emphasis on full employment than on inflation management, using a range of fiscal, monetary, and price-control techniques to obtain the right trade-off between unemployment and inflation. This politically hands-on approach to economic management ran into trouble in the 1970s, as successive oil shocks and rising inflationary expectations produced "stagflation"—an intractable mix of high inflation and high unemployment (a nasty conundrum that the United Kingdom may be facing once again).

The doctrine of central bank independence and the narrow focus on very low inflation are quite recent innovations.

The economic crises of the 1970s gave the Hayekians and their political supporters on the New Right their chance. They blamed the rampant inflation on overly strong unions (which were demanding higher wage settlements) and too much politics. A new breed of economists argued that policymakers will be prone to time-inconsistency: they would promise low inflation but would deliver electorally popular policies that produce too much inflation. The solution, the economists argued, was to get politics out of the picture by not only making central banks autonomous, but also constraining central bankers' discretion through simple rules.

Although there have been a number of variations in this approach over the years, the basic assumptions have remained consistent: if you can limit monetary policy to a set of simple rules and make inflation-fighting the priority, you should be able to create a low-inflation economy. But to make this work, you have to insulate rate-setters from political influence, or all your inflation-fighting credibility will go up in smoke.

Advocates of this system argue that the demands of democratic accountability are met because governments usually choose the objectives that guide central bank policy, even if they must let central banks then decide how to reach them. Yet

the combination of policy autonomy and a very narrow inflation-focused rule dramatically reduces the ability of monetary policymakers to respond to the broad economic needs of the public or the complex demands of a modern economy. Of course, in practice, central bankers have sometimes pursued a more nuanced discretionary policy (as they are arguably doing today). And, of course, they have not always been immune to political pressure. As William Niskanen wrote in his book, Reaganomics, "The Fed is independent in the same way that Finland is independent – by accommodating to the strongest external pressures." Above all, bankers have had to be less than transparent about these facts, further eroding their claim to democratic accountability.

A protestor jumps on the table in front of ECB President Mario Draghi at a press conference in Frankfurt, April 2015.

THE POLITICS OF INFLATION

It is clear that the doctrine of central bank independence defines monetary policy as an issue that should be beyond the vicissitudes of democratic pressure. Yet is this a political move or merely a technical matter of convenience? To see the politics of it, look to the reactions to recent monetary policy by different groups: homeowners and other debtors have been delighted by recent extremely low rates, whereas retirees have been very hard hit by low returns in safe investments.

Monetary policy has a huge impact on the economy as a whole and also produces winners and losers. For example, increasing or lowering interest rates is as distributional as tax policy. It is just more politically opaque when you reward savers and punish borrowers by raising rates. Similarly, policies of quantitative easing are premised upon a wealth effect whereby the asset values of those with the most assets are artificially inflated, rewarding those who already have the most. Given that monetary policy is so politically and distributionally significant, policymakers should provide us with very good reasons for radically limiting democratic oversight. On the surface, those reasons are largely technical, couched in the economic language of time-inconsistency and moral hazard. But underlying this technocratic rationale is a more fundamental fear about the potentially devastating risks of severe inflation.

As the McGill political economist Juliet Johnson argues in her research on central bank museums, when central bankers set out to explain their mission to the general public, they dramatize the danger of inflation. Every bank museum has a display that discusses the risks of inflation, and many try to make those risks real to the visitor— by, for example, demonstrating how rapidly their money declines in value over time with a higher rate of inflation. Underlying these discussions of the problems of moderate inflation, however, is the specter of hyperinflation: just about every central bank museum also has a depiction of the horrors of the German hyperinflation of the 1930s, in which families famously had to push wheelbarrows of cash to buy a loaf of bread, producing the political and economic instability that enabled Hitler's rise to power.

The irony, of course, is that the hyperinflation actually happened in the 1920s and was a deliberate German policy to disrupt reparations to France. It worked in that regard and then was ended by 1924. The suspension of reparations resulted in an economic boom that lasted until 1929, when the world economy fell off a cliff. Hitler came to power in 1933 because of unemployment, but you would never know that from the story central banks tell themselves about 1923. But the story serves a purpose. No matter how remote such a possibility is, it is the fear of hyperinflation that justifies the creation of a technocratic zone of liberal exceptionalism that constrains democratic oversight.

STATE OF EMERGENCY

The technocratic approach to monetary policy seemed to work reasonably well during the Great Moderation—a period of unusual macroeconomic stability that lasted from the mid-1980s until the 2008 financial crisis. But the 2008 global financial crisis changed everything. In their efforts to fight a global financial meltdown and to stave off deflation, central bankers threw out the rule book and started experimenting with a range of unconventional monetary policies.

This is where the second side of exceptionalism began to make an appearance. All of these measures have been framed as temporary, exceptional responses to the serious threat posed by the crisis, and thus operate through the logic of emergency exceptionalism. Here again, we can see the classic elements of exceptionalist politics: the declaration of an existential threat, followed by the suspension of normal politics.

Monetary policy has a huge impact on the economy as a whole and also produces winners and losers.

Although there were countless invocations of an extreme threat, no doubt the most potent was Federal Reserve Chairman Ben Bernanke's infamous statement to lawmakers that without the rapid rollout of emergency measures, "There won't be any economy Monday." In turn, political and economic leaders who relied on technocratic exceptionalism to keep the politics out began to act in a most political manner— bailing out corporations instead of letting them fail, suspending trading on the stock exchanges, nationalizing failing banks, and pushing through enabling legislation where adequate emergency authority did not yet exist.

Central bankers also moved quickly to adopt various exceptional and unconventional policies in response to the crisis. Indeed, most of the unconventional monetary policies that have been tried to date break quite radically with the underlying economic ideas that justify technocratic exclusion in the first place. For example, when exceptionally low interest rates were not providing enough stimulus in recent years, negative interest rates, which weren't even supposed to be economically possible (until they were tried), were applied. Quantitative easing pushes the envelope on what central banks are supposed to never do: print money.

RESPONDING TO ILLIBERALISM

The rule-based approach to monetary policy was supposed to avoid this kind of ad-hoc policymaking, which is why it isn't too surprising that the current monetary order is facing some serious challenges to its legitimacy. Over the past year, the U.S. Federal Reserve's Janet Yellen, the Bank of England's Mark Carney, and the European Central Bank's Mario Draghi have all been criticized for being too political, too powerful, and too unaccountable. Criticizing Carney, for example, became "the new Tory sport" after he warned of the potential economic fallout of a "yes" vote during the Brexit referendum.

Yet central bankers do bear some responsibility for their current woes. Even during the Great Moderation, the underlying exceptionalism of monetary policy had corrosive effects on the institutions' longer-term legitimacy. Monetary policy is always political. It is not just that different interest rate decisions have winners and losers, but that the very focus on low inflation (rather than full employment, growth, or some other economic priority) has political effects, tilting economic policy toward the financial sector and savers in general, and away from working (and borrowing) families.

The narrow focus on inflation also weakened central banks' ability to foresee the financial crisis. As late at the summer of 2007, the Federal Reserve's preoccupation with inflation levels blinded them to the financial instabilities already at work. And, of course, once the financial crisis was in full swing and central bankers began using their emergency powers to respond, the public began to ask how it was that some of the most powerful people in the world were unelected.

These failings are only one part of the bigger picture of economic inequality, crisis, and stagnation that has helped to create the conditions for the rise of illiberal populism—but they do play their part. Moreover, by effectively denying the political implications of their actions, central bankers only became further disconnected from the wider public. And yet the bankers are not entirely to blame for their present predicament either. After all, who tasked them with saving the global economy—not just in the early days of the crisis, but for many long years afterwards? Western politicians passed the buck as quickly as they could, shifting from stimulus to austerity in a few short years and placing the burden for recovery on central banks.

Central bankers and politicians share a common desire: to get the politics out of the process. Unfortunately, it turns out that this is impossible. In fact, recent events make it clear that not only are monetary policies inherently political, but that the very attempt to separate them from political pressures can have the opposite effect. This is the paradox of monetary credibility: although economic theory says that monetary credibility and low inflation depend on getting the politics out, at the end of the day, in a democratic society, credibility also depends on the legitimacy of the monetary system and its institutions to deliver policy that works.

Policymakers' efforts to depoliticize economic policy only work to repress and displace those politics, forcing public concerns out of the formal political system and into far more radical and potentially illiberal areas and ultimately threatening the liberal system that policymakers seek to preserve. This is not to suggest that the denigration of expertise is a justifiable political move, but instead that observers should cultivate a more modest and engaged form of expertise, particularly in areas in which both facts and values are contested—and that definitely includes economics, as the economists Dani Rodrik and Jonathan Kirshner have both eloquently argued.

There are plenty of signs that the old economic certainties of the Great Moderation are gone for good. Yellen and Bank of Canada Governor Stephen Poloz have suggested that simple rules no longer apply in a radically uncertain context. And although Western central bankers continue to declare their allegiance to the golden two percent rule, their actions point in a very different direction (recent interest rate increases in the United States and Canada in spite of declining inflation being a case in point).

In the short term, we may well be relieved to know that the norms of central bank independence and rule-based policy provide a measure of protection from populist tendencies under the Trump administration and elsewhere. But when Trump ideologue Steve Bannon criticizes capitalism for its amorality and invokes the concerns of middle-class and working-class people, all the while defining the alt-right as their champion, we need to come up with a better answer than to encourage people to have faith in the two percent inflation target.

JACQUELINE BEST is Professor in the School of Political Studies at the University of Ottawa and the author of *Governing Failure*.

© Foreign Affairs

Trump and the Bond Market

Why a Flight From U.S. Treasuries Is Unlikely

Sandy Brian Hager

U.S. President Donald Trump and Treasury Secretary Steven Mnuchin at the Treasury Department in Washington, April 2017.

Donald Trump's presidential campaign frightened bond market investors around the world. Trump pledged to slash federal income taxes and spend up to $1 trillion upgrading the United States' infrastructure. Investors worried that his victory would lead to massive federal deficits and runaway inflation, eroding the value of their holdings. The title of an April 2016 article in Forbes captured the mood: "President Donald Trump Would Destroy the Bond Market."

The anxiety was particularly acute among foreign investors, who own around 40 percent of the $14 trillion worth of outstanding U.S. Treasury securities. When

Trump hinted during the campaign that he would "make a deal" with creditors to reduce the value of their Treasuries, pundits asked whether the Chinese and Japanese central banks would begin to sour on the U.S. debt they had been stockpiling as part of their foreign exchange reserves.

To be sure, foreign confidence in U.S. Treasuries had wavered long before the 2016 election. In recent years, budget deficits, quantitative easing, and the political dramas surrounding the debt ceiling and other fiscal issues had put the creditworthiness of the U.S. federal government in doubt. Still, the prospect of Trump's victory introduced a new dynamic altogether, leading some observers to fear that a panicked selloff of Treasury securities could be around the corner.

The stakes were high. The U.S. Treasuries market is the largest and most liquid financial market in the world, and as the world's premier low-risk assets, U.S. Treasuries are a benchmark against which most other assets are priced. U.S. regulators require banks to hold Treasuries as part of the safe assets on their balance sheets, and investors turn to Treasuries as safe havens in uncertain times. Treasuries have also been the linchpin of U.S. global financial power: steady foreign demand for them has allowed the United States to cheaply finance big deficits.

In the week after the November 8 election, around $1 trillion was wiped off of global bond markets as investors moved away from U.S. and other government debt. But that was no panic, and for a few reasons, U.S. Treasuries will probably remain the world's premier risk-free asset. The first is a lack of attractive alternatives from other governments: the U.S. bond market is the best of a questionable batch. The second is that the big companies and superwealthy families in the United States hold a disproportionately large share of the country's domestically owned public debt and would resist policies that would disrupt the bond market.

U.S. President Donald Trump celebrating with Congressional Republicans after the U.S. Congress passed a tax overhaul, Washington, December 2017.

NOWHERE TO RUN

The U.S. economy can seem dysfunctional. But investment decisions are always relative, and compared with the alternatives, U.S. Treasuries look like beacons of stability. There are two challengers that might supplant U.S. Treasuries in the long term—eurozone government debt and Chinese government debt. Neither is especially attractive.

Eurozone bond markets are still reeling from the sovereign debt crisis in southern Europe, driven by Italy's broken banking system and the prospect of a Greek default. The United Kingdom's decision to leave the European Union has cast further doubt on the future of the European project and the monetary union it supports. And unemployment, slow growth, and inequality have created the potential for another populist wave on the continent, which would compromise the security of eurozone government debt.

If not the eurozone, then what about China? As part of its recent financial reforms, Beijing has sought to open up foreign access to China's interbank bond market. The reforms are meant to promote the international use of the renminbi (RMB) and increase China's global financial influence. In November 2015, the International Monetary Fund announced that it would include the RMB alongside the U.S. dollar, the euro, the yen, and the pound sterling in the basket of international currencies used to value the Special Drawing Right.

Yet China has a long way to go before it can rival the United States as the world's top source of safe assets. Investors still fret over China's opaque institutions, its slowing economic growth, its volatile stock market, its use of capital controls, and its growing piles of private and public debt. The size of the Chinese bond market, which is worth about $4 trillion, pales in comparison with that of the U.S. Treasuries market, and foreign ownership of China's public debt remains very low. And despite Beijing's efforts, the RMB's use in international transactions fell between 2015 and 2016 by almost 30 percent. All of this uncertainty reinforces the relatively safe status of the U.S. Treasuries market.

As emerging markets drive global growth in the coming years, the value of the dollar will probably undergo a gradual fall. Central banks in Beijing and Tokyo could limit their losses by selling some of their U.S. Treasuries now. But that too is unlikely, thanks to a dynamic that the economist Eswar Prasad has called the "dollar trap." By selling their Treasuries, Beijing and Tokyo could set off a panicked flight from the Treasuries market—and that would be bad news for big exporters such as China and Japan, since it would further weaken the value of the dollar and make U.S. exports more competitive.

Jason Lee / REUTERS

The headquarters of the People's Bank of China in Beijing, June 2013.

MONEY TALKS

There is another reason that U.S. Treasuries will likely retain their safe status: their powerful domestic owners will seek to protect them.

In recent years, domestic ownership of the United States' public debt has become increasingly unequal: the richest American families and the biggest financial corporations have acquired a disproportionate share of U.S. Treasuries. Among U.S. households, the share of public debt held by the richest one percent climbed from around 20 percent in 1969 to 56 percent in 2013. Meanwhile, in the corporate sector, the top 2,500 companies' share of the debt jumped from 65 percent in the period between 1977 and 1981 to 82 percent in the period between 2006 to 2010. Highly concentrated mutual funds have expanded their holdings of U.S. Treasuries as pension funds, which are more widely held, have lost some of their share. All of this has aligned the interests of the richest Americans with those of the biggest financial firms.

This concentration of public debt is the result of the four-decade evolution of what the economic sociologist Wolfgang Streeck has called the "debt state." In the case of the United States, rising federal spending and stagnating federal revenues—themselves a result of increasingly regressive tax policies—have produced ever-deeper levels of public debt. The United States' wealthies families and biggest companies have waged a successful political battle to reduce their tax burdens; they now pay less tax relative to their income than they did a few decades ago. That has produced more inequality—and more savings for the rich to invest in rising public debt. In effect, the federal government is borrowing from powerful domestic groups instead of taxing them. If Trump ever seriously threatened he safe status of U.S. Treasury securities, these powerful domestic owners would probably rise up in opposition.

At this point, there are few signs that Trump will try to disrupt the debt state. To the contrary: the tax reforms backed by his administration could add up to $1.5 trillion to the deficit over the next decade. Because the bulk of the tax cuts will benefit top earners, the reforms would further entrench the power of domestic groups with interests in a stable Treasuries market.

IN THE LONG RUN

This assessment applies only to the short term. In the longer run, a financial crash, a natural disaster, domestic unrest, or a major war could quickly bring about systemic changes, unraveling the global financial order and ending the U.S. Treasury market's role as a safe haven. More optimistically, Trump could deliver a sustained economic recovery, reducing the U.S. deficit and placing the onus on other governments to supply the global financial system with safe assets. Wouldn't that, too, disrupt the position of U.S. Treasuries?

Perhaps. But there is reason to be skeptical of Washington's ability to produce such an outcome. First, Trump's proposals for recovery have hinged mainly on his pledge to increase infrastructure spending. With such large tax cuts in the offing, however, it is unlikely that Republicans will throw their support behind an expensive infrastructure plan. Second, Trump's fiscal strategy appears to contradict the other component of his blueprint for growth: a weaker dollar. Increased deficit spending could lead to rising interest rates, which attract capital inflows. To the detriment of U.S. exporters, those inflows would strengthen the dollar and widen the current account deficit far more than the tax cuts would on their own.

Nor is this all. The political economists Shimshon Bichler and Jonathan Nitzan have shown that since the 1940s, rising employment rates tend to be followed by falling pretax corporate profits and falling stock prices relative to wages. Unemployment is already falling, and if Trump delivers on his promises to create even more jobs, profits and the stock market would fall even further than they would otherwise. Having appointed the wealthiest cabinet in U.S. history, Trump will likely be reluctant to aggressively pursue policies with such potentially detrimental consequences for the superrich.

Domestic ownership of the United States' public debt has become increasingly unequal.

Bichler and Nitzan identify yet another factor that might dampen enthusiasm for a Trump-style recovery: the effect of employment growth on interest rates. Since the 1960s, they note, "employment growth has become a nearly perfect five-year leading predictor for interest rates." As employment rose in the 1960s and 1970s, interest rates climbed; since the early 1980s, both employment growth and interest rates have fallen. Substantial growth in employment today could send interest rates soaring and bring an end to the bull market that cheap credit has encouraged.

Trump's election made investors justifiably nervous. But a mass exodus from the U.S. Treasuries market is unlikely, both because the United States remains the most relatively safe investment option in a perilous world and because Trump's policies will entrench the power of the superrich owners of Treasuries. The existence of an influential bloc of domestic owners should offer some solace to foreign investors rattled by the new administration's nationalist rhetoric. But perhaps the main lesson for the holders of U.S. Treasuries is that the inertia in the global financial system is strong—even in the face of a change like Trump.

SANDY BRIAN HAGER is a Lecturer in International Political Economy at City, University of London.

The Euro in Decline?

How the Currency Could Spoil the Global Financial System

Kathleen R. McNamara

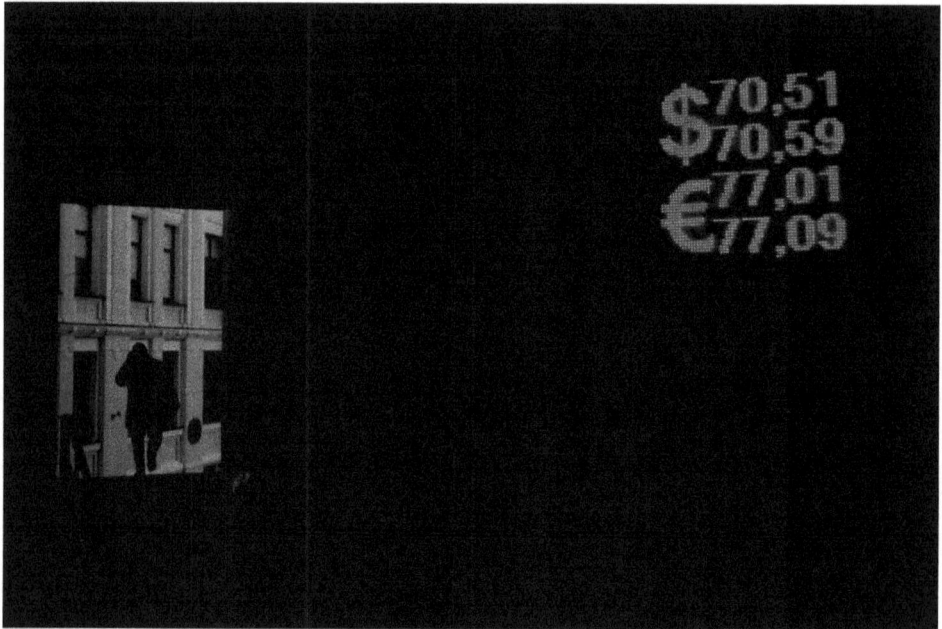

A board with the currency exchange rates of the U.S. dollar and the Euro, March 10, 2016.

When the euro was created some 15 years ago, there was speculation that the new currency might come to challenge the dominance of the U.S. dollar as the international reserve currency of choice. But the euro's guardian, the European Central Bank (ECB), had little appetite for such a role. Likewise, foreign exchange markets showed little support for supplanting the dollar's hegemony with the euro, despite a move into euro-denominated bonds and a strengthening of the value of the euro over the 2000s. This has meant that the EU has, in large part, played a "helper" role in U.S. financial hegemony throughout the postwar era to today.

But now, Europe's "helper" status may well be in question. The populist forces that have emerged throughout the continent challenge the legitimacy of the euro and threaten both the institutional and ideational foundations upon which it rests. With this uncertainty arises the possibility of the EU turning into a "risk generator" within the global financial order or perhaps even worse—a "spoiler" of the very system itself.

AN INCOMPLETE POLITICAL DEVELOPMENT

The sovereign authority of the ECB is critical to the broader stability of the global financial system. But one of its key weaknesses involves the particularities of the euro's design: unlike every other successful single currency, the ECB stands by itself at the European level, without the broader societal and political institutions needed to give currencies a solid and durable foundation. There are four roles in which this broad structure of political authority is needed: to serve as a trusted generator of market confidence and liquidity, to provide robust regulation of financial risk, to build mechanisms for fiscal redistribution and economic adjustment, and to create the political solidarity necessary to undergird hard times. It is this lack of broader governance that places the euro in jeopardy and creates its "spoiler" potential for the international financial system, not its shortcomings as an optimum currency, as some economists such as Paul Krugman have argued.

Regarding the first element—serving as a visible and ironclad backstop to reassure financial markets—the eurozone is doing relatively well. Although originally founded as a hyper-independent central bank and given a narrow mandate to fight inflation and protect the value of the euro, the ECB has proven more innovative in providing confidence and liquidity over time than imagined by its creators when they met in Maastricht in the early 1990s. Most notably, the ECB, under the leadership of Mario Draghi, has issued hundreds of billions of euros in emergency loans to European banks over the years following the implosion of the Greek economy in the wake of the 2008 global recession. The policy to some extent mirrored the U.S. Treasury and Federal Reserve's decision in 2008 to bail out American banks through the Troubled Assets Relief Program. The ECB's Long Term Refinancing Operations, which lends money at very low interest rates to troubled member states, was also a significant departure from the ECB's image as an institution that would not act to backstop entities in financial distress. LTROS have proven relatively successful in calming markets and giving indebted member states some breathing room to reform—even as policy demands for austerity have been severely damaging.

These new policies and programs have been matched by a much more forceful and overtly political set of statements from the ECB leadership. In the summer of 2012, Draghi's muscular remarks pledging his institution to do "whatever it takes" to save the euro got plenty of attention across Europe and the United States, but it was only one of many such statements that came from the ECB over the course of the eurozone crisis. In terms of both its institutional capacity and its role in the political debate, the ECB has been playing a critical and unexpected role as an unofficial lender of last resort and thus reducing the EU's role as a potential "risk generator."

The second factor, however, which requires a European banking and financial union, is where the EU has shown more weakness. The deep financial integration across European states demands an overarching framework to protect against a contagion of banking crises. Although there has been some movement toward such a banking union framework, it remains unfinished. The European Commission, with support from the ECB, has been successful in getting an agreement on a single supervisory mechanism for the eurozone's banks. This initiative is spearheaded by the ECB and provides a single rulebook for all banks. The European Banking Authority, created in 2011, is an important new actor regulating eurozone and non-euro states as part of the European System of Financial Supervision. These regulatory and institutional developments, however, have yet to include crucial elements such as common deposit insurance, which would protect against a cataclysmic run on the banks across the EU, and bank resolution rules have yet to be implemented to deal with future banking crises.

The third element—fiscal and economic union—remains the most far out of reach for the EU. Although some have argued that the EU only needs the politically more feasible banking union, fiscal union remains critical to managing the inevitable slings and arrows of a shared currency by providing mechanisms for fiscal redistribution and economic adjustment. A fiscal union involves the ability to extract revenue through taxes, to redistribute money through public spending, and to raise additional funds through public debt instruments. The EU currently has none of these explicit functions, although it does (less visibly) redistribute funds through its European Regional Development Fund and the European Social Fund. Proposals for "eurobonds" and other ways to mutualize debt in the eurozone have proved politically inflammatory because they smack of much deeper political integration than many in Europe are willing to accept while giving some in Germany the fear that they will be on the hook for profligate spending by their neighbors. In lieu of a fiscal union, the EU's leadership and the heads of state and government have aggressively sought to impose austerity programs, involving deficit and debt reduction, on societies that are still reeling from the fallout of the financial crisis. Such efforts look much more like the IMF's conditional lending programs and structural adjustment loans than an embedded governance system that could hold together a monetary union. These austerity programs jeopardize the EU's future and, thus, stability in the broader global financial order.

Finally, the EU is also missing a broader political union, which is the legitimating foundation for all other currencies. Although the EU has become remarkably institutionalized over the past 50 years, with a constitutional-like legal framework and a series of politics and practices that deeply affect the everyday lives of all Europeans, it does not have all the state-like governance structures that support all other national currencies. To the detriment of European and global stability, the EU simply has not created the social solidarity and the legitimate political institutions to adequately embed the euro in a larger political framework.

Because the political mechanisms for stabilizing the European economy remain elusive, the crises of refugee flows and migrant resettlement, Brexit, and the rise of populist anti-EU groups has cast serious doubt on the larger European project and with it has transformed Europe's role as a "helper" into that of a "risk generator" in the global financial order.

THE DECLINE OF NEOLIBERALISM

But institutional configurations are not the only important factor in considering the security of the EU's role in the global financial order. Ideas are critical and unavoidable legitimating devices, too. In fact, the hyper-independent, politically-insulated ECB is itself partly the result of the broader culture of neoliberalism, a set of ideas that encompasses a range of policies, such as the strict delegation of control over the money supply to experts who are delinked from representative democracy. The theoretical rationale behind this idea is straightforward: politicians chasing votes are likely to try to manipulate the economy in ways that make the populace happy in the short term, disregarding the potential for their monetary policies to produce economic trouble in the long run. The insulation of central banks from the direct influence of elected officials was one of the most notable governance changes globally in the 1990s. The ECB, established in 1999, took central bank independence to the extreme, with only weak channels of political representation and oversight.

Central bank independence achieved a formidable status in contemporary political life, with little questioning of its logic or effectiveness. But the evidence in support of central bank independence has always been mixed at best. This contradiction can be explained by what I call the spread of a "rational fiction." Governments such as those in the eurozone choose to delegate financial power to acquire important legitimizing and symbolic properties, which are particularly attractive in times of uncertainty or economic distress.

This dynamic is rational and instrumental, but only when placed within a very specific cultural and historical context that legitimizes that delegation—the culture of neoliberalism. But moving to an independent central bank only appears to shelter monetary policy from politics. In fact, as Jacqueline Best has argued in Foreign Affairs, it solidifies a specific set of ideologies and partisan positions that favor certain societal groups, most notably investors, over others, such as workers. The ECB benefited from the strong consensus about the desirability of central bank independence that was part and parcel of the neoliberal turn of the 1990s onward.

The question is this: after several decades of low inflation and slow growth, will this independent central bank legitimating dynamic hold? This is far from clear, as the disastrous effects of the austerity policies imposed on debtor countries such as Greece, Ireland, Italy, Portugal, and Spain have created deep political cleavages and fanned the flames of populist backlash against the insulated EU technocracy. As euroskeptic parties emerge across the EU to challenge the orthodox liberal consensus that ruled the EU, it is unclear whether the legitimating foundations of the ECB and the euro still hold today. If the justification for the ECB's independence is challenged but the institutional configuration of the EU is not updated to lend the euro the political authority it needs, the chances are high that the EU will struggle mightily.

Just as observers now fear that the United States is in a structurally weakened position because of President Donald Trump's seeming rejection of the United States' "indispensable nation" role, the incomplete political development of the EU and the backlash against the ECB's legitimating ideology bring into question Europe's ability to navigate future crises. These factors make the EU a "risk generator" at the very least and a potential "spoiler" in the global financial order at worst. The global financial system can ill afford such an outcome.

How the Eurozone Might Split

Could Germany Become a Reluctant Hegemon?

Mark Blyth and Simon Tilford

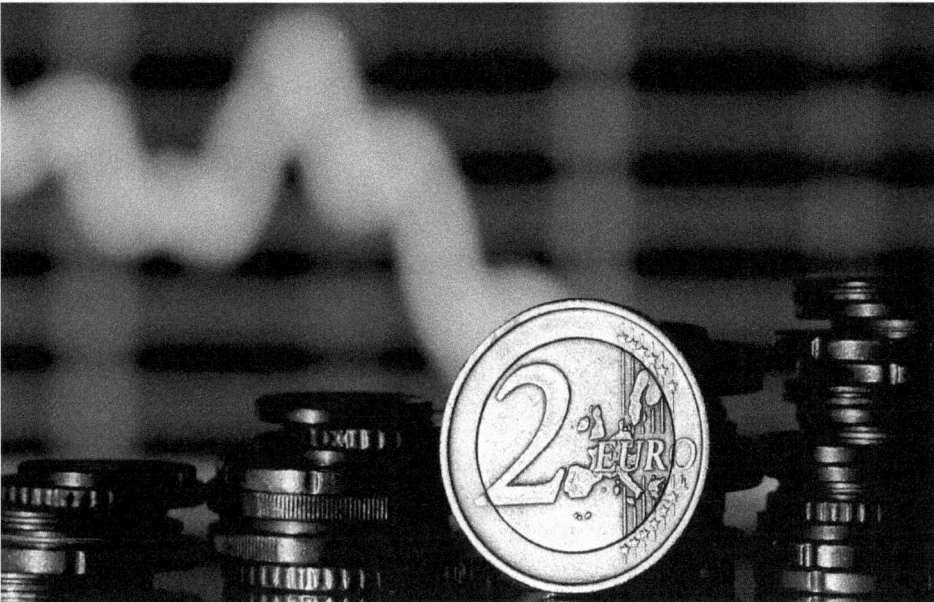

Euro coins on display in Zenica, Bosnia and Herzegovina, June 2015.

In February 2016, the Organization for Economic Cooperation and Development opined that developed country growth prospects had "practically flat-lined" and that only a stronger "commitment to raising public investment would boost demand and help support future growth." Fast-forward some 24 months, and despite Brexit, the election of U.S. President Donald Trump, and the rise of the populist Alternative für Deutschland in Germany, the euro seems to be a much better bet than it has been in a long time. But has the euro really weathered the crisis and come out stronger? In this article, we make two interrelated arguments about the future of the eurozone.

The first is that even if the recent economic upturn continues, the eurozone could still split in two over the medium to long term thanks to a built-in design flaw in the eurozone architecture that makes it extremely difficult for the eurozone governors to deal with persistent export and import imbalances between states.

As a single-currency area, the eurozone formally has no internal imbalances. In reality, however, the persistent export surpluses it runs against the rest of the world are generated in the north and east of the eurozone, while persistent budget deficits are generated in the south, an imbalance that could yet lead to a split in the eurozone. This would result in Germany and the eastern European states keeping the euro even if France and the southern Europeans bail out. Europe would be left with two sets of countries: those in the core of the eurozone, largely in northern and eastern Europe, that would remain on the euro (or "real euro") and those in the south that would be pushed to adopt a new currency, which we term the "nuevo euro." (The nuevo euro countries would be unlikely to revert to their pre-euro national currencies for fear of adding to the already grave disruption caused by their break with the real euro.)

Such a split would be massively disruptive. As investors came to fear a devaluation of the nuevo euro, assets denominated in real euros would instantly become more valuable. The banking systems of nuevo euro countries would implode owing to capital flight, and the currency would plunge in value. Most important, the resulting flood of capital into core Europe would cause the value of the real euro to rise dramatically, damaging these countries' all-important exports.

In such a world, countries on the real euro would be forced to adopt the United States' strategy of debt management. Once the nuevo euro had stabilized at a lower real effective exchange rate (REER), investors from nuevo euro countries would want to hold real euro assets—in particular real euro government bonds—as insurance against further depreciation of their own currency. As a hedge against further devaluation, nuevo euro investors would be willing to accept very low returns on their real euro assets, much the way European investors currently hold low-interest Swiss assets and Asian countries hold U.S. Treasury bills. And just as the United States has done over the past 30 years, real euro countries could in turn invest the proceeds of these bond sales abroad in search of higher returns.

In order to pursue these returns, however, the real euro countries would open themselves up to the significant risk of their new external investments losing value because of a currency shock or other crisis. Although the United States can cope with such shocks given its size and the fact that it prints its own currency, thus making its debt problems more manageable, Germany and other real euro countries would enjoy no such luxury. By accumulating such assets, they would be exposing themselves to very large capital losses (relative to their GDP) in the event of a market shock. And since these countries have no ability to print money in order to bail out those holding such assets, a shock could be seriously disruptive. As such, real euro countries would likely resist such a buildup of external assets, preferring instead to allow their currency to appreciate strongly, at least until that really began to impact their exports.

Taken together, this would lead the real euro countries, especially Germany, to become a European version of the United States, albeit without the latter's famous "exorbitant privilege," whereby the United States gets to print the reserve currency, dollars, that everyone else has to earn in order to conduct foreign exchange. For the real euro countries, although their currency would be a reserve asset for nuevo euro investors, it wouldn't buy them the "free lunch" that the United States gets from printing the dollar. Rather, it would merely expose them to more risk on their excess foreign assets.

Our second argument is that in the short to medium term, even if the eurozone generates enough growth to avoid such a split, populism in Europe remains alive and well. A populist electoral victory resulting in a Brexit-style referendum on the euro somewhere in the eurozone therefore cannot be ruled out entirely. If such a referendum was to pass, it would lead to the same capital flight and REER appreciation detailed above, albeit through a slightly different pathway. In short, for reasons of both long-term sustainability and short-term politics, the euro is not out of the woods yet.

Ralph Orlowski / Reuters

The ECB headquarters in Frankfurt, January 2018.

ASIAN FUSION

The narrative emanating from Brussels since the start of 2017 is that with an increasingly robust economic recovery, all is returning to normal. Forecasts do indeed look brighter than they have for a decade, and, politically speaking, the French and Dutch general elections both saw defeats for populists, suggesting that the center will hold. This narrative is reassuring. Given recent populist electoral successes in Austria,

Germany, and the Czech Republic, however, and the looming Italian elections with several anti-euro parties in the mix, it could be complacent. As such, and despite the turn to growth, the euro's future is by no means secure. A comparison of Europe's financial crisis and aftermath with what happened in Asia a decade ago shows why this is the case.

In the 1990s, a number of Asian countries received large capital inflows from the developed world as part of that decade's mania for emerging markets. Indonesia, Malaysia, Thailand, and South Korea, like peripheral eurozone countries in the first decade of the twenty-first century, were places where developed world investors could seek higher rates of return than were available in their own countries. As a result, these Asian states accumulated liabilities in foreign currencies, mostly dollars, that took the form of government bond purchases and external lines of dollar-denominated credit. When liquidity evaporated in 1997, they were unable to print the money to pay their debts. To avoid a repeat of this fiasco, all the countries affected by the crisis began, by 1999, to run structural export surpluses and accumulate massive foreign exchange reserves as insurance against future shocks.

In response to its own crisis in 2011, Europe pulled the same macroeconomic trick. Between 2001 and 2016, according to data from Haver Analytics, the eurozone shifted from a trade surplus of under one percent of GDP to one of close to 3.5 percent. But although the entire eurozone's export surplus in the first quarter of 2017 was 90.9 billion euros, 65.9 billion of that surplus against the rest of the world came from Germany alone. Germany may be legendarily efficient, but how does less than 30 percent of the eurozone generate over 70 percent of the surplus? The answer points to a structural tension that could prove to be the real undoing of the euro.

In the first decade of the twenty-first century, central and eastern European economies ran large current account deficits—that is, they imported more than they exported. These deficits were driven by an influx of capital from Germany, as German export firms invested in rebuilding the capital stocks of these central and eastern European countries and integrating them into German supply chains. Because most of this was equity investment in the form of plant and equipment, and in moving plant and equipment to eastern Europe from Germany, and since equity is more resistant to shocks than debt, once global export markets recovered after 2011, these economies boomed. According to our own calculations based on data from the UN and the Atlas of Economic Complexity, an average of 25 percent of the exports of Austria, the Czech Republic, Hungary, Poland, Romania, Slovakia, and Slovenia go straight to Germany. Like East Asia a decade before, these countries now run structural trade surpluses and rely on tight public spending at home to keep costs down and exports competitive. But what about other countries in Europe, such as France, Italy, and Spain, whose growth models are much more dependent upon internal consumption and domestic demand, and for whom the budgetary squeeze in the years following the financial crisis contributed to extremely low growth or no growth at all? Can they too profit from austerity-driven exports?

Even if the recent economic upturn continues, the eurozone could still split.

AN ABUSIVE RELATIONSHIP

The short answer is "No." Italy has barely grown in over a decade and is now running a small external trade surplus. Spain has gone from a trade deficit of around ten percent in 2007 to a surplus today of around two percent. The big outlier in the eurozone is France, which used to run a trade surplus but now runs twin budget and trade deficits of around 3.5 and 2 percent, respectively. Given the common eurozone pressures to export one's way to growth, the result of the eurozone governments collectively doing too little to boost domestic demand, both France and the other larger consumption-led states will have little option but to try to improve their trade competitiveness over the next few years and grow through exports. Spain has been able to do so, but mainly because imports have fallen as consumption declined and unemployment rose, depressing labor costs and improving export competitiveness. Italy is stuck.

This amounts to a structural problem. The Germans and the central and eastern Europeans are running an export surplus against the rest of the eurozone, and at the end of the day all surpluses and deficits must sum to zero. But the EU's fiscal framework makes it hard for eurozone countries such as France to run budget deficits to offset the depressing impact on their economies of their trade deficits with the rest of the eurozone. The resulting message to these countries—you must engage in ongoing austerity so the Germans and others in northern and central Europe can grow—is populist dynamite, because in such a world permanent austerity becomes the government's de facto policy regardless of whom you vote for.

This arrangement creates the obvious risk that France, or more likely Italy, will eventually elect a populist government. Emmanuel Macron's victory in the French presidential election in May was seen as a rejection of populism, but he has yet to persuade the Germans to agree to the deep eurozone reforms necessary for his agenda to move forward, and it is doubtful that he will be able to do so. If Macron fails, the next French president could be a populist of the left or right committed to holding a referendum on French membership in the eurozone. Meanwhile the Italian economy is still in deep trouble. At its current rate of growth, between one and 1.5 percent, it will take several more years for it to return to its 2007 size, and its banking system is a mess. The next Italian general election, or the one after that, could still bring a party into government intent on calling a referendum on the euro. What would happen then?

The threat of France or Italy (or both) leaving the euro could, in theory, prompt Germany and its allies to accept a substantive pooling of risk within the eurozone to head off any exit, perhaps through the issuance of common eurozone debt or a combination of large-scale debt write-downs and more expansionary fiscal policies, which would help the debt-burdened countries of southern Europe. Doing so, however, would require a seismic shift on the part of the Germans, who have staked out a position based on austerity and fiscal discipline. Indeed, it is more likely that the German government will double down on existing policy. By doing so, however, it will make these eurozone referendums all the more likely.

If a referendum in France or Italy went ahead, the outcome would not really matter, as the simple announcement of such a vote would prompt investors to move their deposits from the referendum country's banks—and possibly those of every other peripheral EU state—into banks in Germany and other core European states to guard against devaluation. The scale of this capital outflow would dwarf the ability of the European Central Bank (ECB), let alone local banks and governments, to stabilize the situation. And even if states tried to stem this outflow through the imposition of capital controls, this very imposition would effectively sound the death knell for the currency union. Although the process would be hugely disruptive, eventually a core group of countries would emerge, based around Germany, that remained on the original euro, at the same time as more peripheral states such as France, Greece, Italy, and Spain adopted a weaker currency, the nuevo euro.

A RELUCTANT HEGEMON

Such a split would be especially difficult for Germany. First, yields on German accounts would fall sharply as the country's banks pushed down interest rates in order to deter further capital flight into the country. The influx of cash would cause the real euro to appreciate, and although Germany could simply allow this to happen until real euros became expensive enough to deter the purchase of German assets, such a rise in value would massively disadvantage the exports of the real euro countries. In all likelihood, Germany and its allies would suffer a precipitous drop in exports and industrial production, while the strength of the real euro would push down German inflation as the price of imports dropped, compounding pressures on the country's banks. Germany would thus be faced with an invidious choice—the reluctant hegemon's dilemma. It could either learn to cope with a hugely overvalued currency and deflation or issue tons of new sovereign debt to soak up foreign demand for its assets.

There is currently a shortage of German sovereign debt because the country is running a sizable budget surplus and the ECB is buying up much of whatever debt is available as part of its program of quantitative easing. But in this scenario, with exports and domestic production taking a massive hit as a result of a eurozone split, a large debt-financed fiscal stimulus would be much more appealing, even in Germany.

Of course, Germany would have to run sizable fiscal deficits on an ongoing basis in order to satisfy foreigners' desire to hold German government debt, and not just as a temporary response to an economic shock, which could be a hard policy to follow even if it allowed exports to recover.

Francois Lenoir / Reuters

Greek Finance Minister Yanis Varoufakis, an anti-austerity advocate, speaks with IMF Managing Director Christine Lagarde in Luxembourg, June 2015.

FINIS GERMANIA

Faced with such a dilemma, Germany will not be able to pull off the United States' trick of accommodating huge demand for its debt without suffering much upward pressure on its REER. The German economy is only one-fifth the size of the U.S. economy, which means that Germany will never be able to issue as many bonds as the United States does Treasury securities. And unfortunately for Germany, this flight into German assets could be happening at precisely the time that the Trump administration is making investors question how safe U.S. assets are relative to German ones.

If investors began to flee U.S. bonds, the pressures on Germany would become global. It would be expected to act like a local hegemon—issuing debt and buying external assets with the proceeds, as the United States does today. But unlike the United States, it would get little of the upside from doing so, such as paying significantly lower returns to foreigners than it earns on its foreign assets. Specifically, in order to prevent the value of its currency from rising to dangerous levels, Germany would have to allow its external balance sheet (the assets it buys abroad with the proceeds it gets from selling all those new bonds) to balloon. Germany would simultaneously experience a combination of a very sizable currency appreciation anda very large increase in its exposure to external risk.

In the long term, such a combination of outcomes would not be uniformly bad. Export competitiveness would take a hit, but the flip side would be a big boost to domestic consumption as the prices of imported goods and services fell. This would in turn help rebalance these economies away from their dependence on exports. But as a country with a big surplus of external assets over liabilities, Germany already has significant exposure to foreign risk, which would only increase in this scenario. Moreover, Germany has a poor record of choosing which foreign assets to invest in. German banks have tended to either recycle the country's excess savings into low-risk, low-return, fixed income assets abroad or lend them to foreign banks. Unlike U.S. banks, they have generally not invested in equities and other high-earning assets. As a result, the Germans have earned disappointingly low returns on their foreign assets when times were good and suffered losses when (as in the pre-euro period) the mark appreciated in real terms or (after the introduction of the euro) financial and fiscal crises reduced the value of its external assets.

If Germany is to enjoy some quasi-hegemonic exorbitant privilege, then it will have to become much better at generating returns on its foreign assets during the good times. What, then, would be the likely balance of privilege and burden for Germany after a messy eurozone breakup?

If investors began to flee U.S. bonds, the pressures on Germany would become global.

Given the size of its economy, Germany's foreign risk, relative to its GDP, would quickly come to exceed that of the United States, meaning that it would suffer much more in any future global economic or financial crisis. Germany would have to accommodate a much sharper real appreciation of its currency than would the United States in the event of a crisis, and its success in doing so would depend to a large extent on whether it embraced structural changes toward more consumption-led growth or resisted this shift and tried to defend its export-led model. Put another way, Germany would have to choose between becoming a kind of enlightened regional economic hegemon and doubling down on its export-driven mercantilism. The challenges facing the central and eastern European economies sharing Germany's currency would be even starker, as demand for their exports would be more sensitive to an appreciation of real euros.

A NEW HOPE?

A eurozone breakup would undoubtedly be disruptive for Europe, but it wouldn't necessarily be all bad. Such an unraveling would force Germany and other states with large structural current-account surpluses to rebalance their economies. To contain their exposure to foreign assets, they would have no choice but to allow their currency to appreciate, hitting exports and boosting domestic consumption. And their need to provide safe assets without igniting an explosion in the size of their banks' balance sheets would force them to issue more debt, reversing the unnecessary austerity that has wreaked so much damage in the eurozone since the onset of the financial crisis. The countries with excess savings—those using real euros—would be left to address the deflation problem they have done much to create, rather than force indebted countries to deal with it through punishing internal devaluations, as they do at present. The problem is how to get there from here without destroying the EU.

It might be possible to engineer such a split by design, but that would require a high degree of cooperation between participating countries and unprecedented dexterity by the ECB together with the national central banks. Moreover, there is little political will for such a move. But in all likelihood, if a single country was to call a referendum on its membership in the eurozone, it would destabilize the power relationships that underpin the EU. This would be a tragedy. The EU badly mishandled the eurozone crisis and appears to be in denial about the scale of the challenges it faces. But the EU still provides the best hope of reconciling globalization with the requirements of national politics.

All of which brings us full circle. The creators of the euro burdened Europe with a currency that can realize its full potential only with a degree of political integration that appears beyond the ability of its participating countries. Yet it is also all but impossible to dismantle the eurozone without imperiling the EU and, with it, political stability in Europe. As we have argued, growth within an unbalanced union can still lead to a split, with populism the trigger. If that happens, Germany's likely inability to play the role of regional hegemon would make the U.S. dollar ever more indispensable and the U.S. economy still more central to the global one, even if it does shift to more overtly antiglobalist policies under Trump. Indeed, German weakness might ultimately be what allows the current system to continue on, despite the best efforts of those in Washington.

MARK BLYTH is Eastman Professor of Political Economy at Brown University. SIMON TILFORD is Chief Economist at the Tony Blair Institute.

Can China Internationalize the RMB?

Lessons From Japan

Saori N. Katada

A woman holds 100-RMB notes at the Bank of China tower in Hong Kong, February 2016.

The jury is still out on whether the Chinese renminbi (RMB) will displace the U.S. dollar in the foreseeable future. What is clear, however, is that challenging a hegemonic currency is not simple. For the RMB to eventually reign supreme, not only would the Chinese leadership, particularly the country's monetary authority, need the political will to prioritize the internationalization of its currency over concerns with domestic stability, it would also have to gain the support of the financial markets and other economic and political players. All that is easier said than done.

The recent history of how the Japanese yen tried and failed to become the dominant international currency provides a good illustration of the challenges. By the late 1980s, the world had started to see Japan's economic power and its currency, the yen, as a major competitor to the U.S. economic order. But Japan was not ready to take on the role of challenger; after the Asian financial crisis (1997–98), the Japanese government made serious efforts to internationalize the yen, but its policies did not help in that regard.

Two decades later, after the Japanese fully liberalized capital account transactions, the yen is largely governed by market forces and is no longer a threat to dollar dominance. Instead, Japan is an effective supporter of dollar-dominated Asia and, given its economic size and its developed financial and monetary capacity, it continues to have great influence in East Asia's economic order. Still, as the region's economic integration deepens and China's currency ambitions increase, Japan also engages in a hedging strategy meant to protect against volatility in the U.S. economy. What Japan does today and the limits of what Japan found it could do in the past tell us a lot about the dynamics of the international monetary order as a whole—and about what China can expect in the coming decades.

JAPAN IN A DOLLAR WORLD

For several decades after the end of World War II, Japan supported dollar dominance in East Asia, partly out of necessity—it relied heavily on exports to the United States and depended on importing natural resources such as petroleum—and partly because of its inefficient domestic financial sector and the government's desire to protect it.

Even when the Japanese yen began to capture headlines for its increasing might in the late 1980s and early 1990s, and despite the abolishment in 1980 of a law that restricted foreign exchange and foreign investment, the Japanese government was neither prepared nor willing to take the necessary steps to make the yen become a rival to the dollar. At that point, the Japanese government saw its control over domestic monetary policy as more important than its ambition for regional currency dominance.

It was only in the aftermath of the 1997 Asian financial crisis that the Japanese government began adopting policies to increase the yen's use in the region as a way of reducing its foreign exchange risk. Policymakers believed that the fundamental cause of the Asian financial crisis was a "double mismatch" in investing in the region. The first mismatch was that short-term investments from external regional actors, particularly the United States, were used to finance long-term projects (a maturity mismatch). The second was that these investments came in the form of U.S. dollars, which were used for local currency funding needs (a currency mismatch).

As the region developed dense production and trade networks with Japan before and after the crisis, balancing dollar dominance by promoting the yen was considered a crucial way to stabilize the region's currency structure. The other motivation was, of course, to use financial stimuli to revive the stagnant Japanese economy after the burst of the economic bubble in the early 1990s. Indeed, the Japanese government revealed its ambition to make Tokyo the region's largest financial center. After 1999, furthermore, the government opted to exempt non-residents from tax withholding on interest and capital gains to facilitate their entry into the market and to improve bond market liquidity and the country's payment settlement system—all to further internationalize the yen.

Tokyo, August 2009.

It is now clear that Japan failed in its ambitions; between 2001 and 2016, the use of the Japanese yen as a reserve currency actually declined from 5.5 percent of total official exchange reserves in the world, according to the IMF, to around three percent. Even in Japan's own trade with the rest of the world, the use of the yen barely increased in exports—from 36.1 percent in 2000 to 37.1 percent in 2016—and imports—from 23.5 percent to 26.1 percent. On the financial center front, Tokyo could never quite catch up to Hong Kong and Singapore. Although Japan continues to be a major creditor in the world and the yen continues to be an important international currency, its presence in the region has decreased, particularly with the rise of the RMB. Arguably, the only major achievement of Tokyo's policy efforts was financial integration with the rest of the world: Japan saw an increase in foreign financial presence through mergers and acquisitions and through carry trade and inward portfolio investment.

Japan failed to make the yen the dominant currency in the region for many reasons. First, the dollar was already dominant. Many developing Asian economies, which experienced large foreign exchange rate fluctuations after the Asian financial crisis, gradually moved to shadow the U.S. dollar (and later the RMB, which moved closely with the dollar). But none shadowed the yen. Second, Japanese financial institutions themselves resisted the move away from their traditional business model, in which they earned large profits through currency hedging between the dollar and the yen. Although changes in Japan's regulatory and institutional environment prepared Japan for yen internationalization, in other words, market players did not follow the government's lead.

The third reason was the persistence of an export-promotion model in East Asia (including Japan) that was largely oriented toward the United States and involved denominating the sales of exports in the currency of the market country. The final sources of failure were Japan's overall economic decline (including a contraction of the Tokyo financial market) and the rise of China, whose rapidly expanding economy made it reluctant to commit to a new regional currency regime dominated by another country.

In the end, the dollar has continued to serve as the regional currency of choice. In the ten years after the Asian financial crisis, the local currency-U.S. dollar hedging market boomed. Meanwhile, despite the establishment of an emergency funding mechanism, called the Chiang Mai Initiative, to fend off currency attacks in Asia, foreign exchange reserves, largely denominated in dollars, have grown—especially in China.

BETWEEN THE RMB AND THE DOLLAR

In the late 2000s, concerns over dollar dominance in East Asia reemerged, this time in the context of the global financial crisis. A widely cited speech delivered by Peoples' Bank of China Governor Zhou Xiaochuan in March 2009 is revealing. In it, Zhou promoted the use of Special Drawing Rights (SDR), the reserve asset created by the IMF, to launch a new global reserve system to replace the current dollar-based one. His plea showcased a fundamental anxiety on the part of East Asian leaders about their dependence on a currency and economy that was proving more tumultuous than expected. The region withstood the crisis quite well, however, protected by a total of $3 trillion in foreign exchange reserves in the hands of East Asian central banks. But with a majority of this reserve invested in short-term dollar-denominated assets such as U.S. treasury bills, and with large holdings of other dollar-denominated assets, Asia would have had a lot to lose.

In the end, the dollar has continued to serve as Asia's currency of choice.

This crisis spurred China's efforts to internationalize the RMB, already gradually underway since the early 2000s. How did Japan react to China's acceleration? On balance, Japan has been lukewarm toward RMB internationalization for the last several years. Japanese non-financial corporations, especially small and medium-sized firms, do not typically use the RMB to settle their trade with China despite the high volume of trade between the two countries. That is in part because using the currency is cumbersome and inconvenient, although with some improvements and a push by China, RMB use in Japan's trade rose in 2015.

Yet Japanese financial institutions, especially globalized mega-banks, remain ambivalent. On the one hand, they see that RMB internationalization will expand their business opportunities overseas. Some, including economists from respected think tanks such as the Namura Research Institute and Japan Research Institute, even argue that doing so would revive Tokyo as a financial center and, by directly trading between the RMB and the yen, might also contribute to the internationalization of the yen. On the other hand, the Japanese financial sector continues to see high risk in the RMB business, stemming from Japan's experience with China's highly politicized financial dealings. The collapse of China's Guangdong International Trust and Investment Corporation (GITIC) in 1999 and Dairen International Trust and Investment Corporation (DITIC) in 2000 forced Japanese banks to forgo most of their outstanding debts.

On the government side, enthusiasm about facilitating the use of RMB around Japan and in Asia has been muted since the early days of RMB internationalization, most likely because of the lack of bottom-up demand from Japan's private sector and a wealth of other priorities. In the early days of China's efforts to internationalize its currency, at a summit between the two countries' leaders, the Japanese government did set up a Japanese-Chinese agreement: "Enhanced Cooperation for Financial Markets Development." The agreement aimed to promote the use of the Japanese yen and RMB in cross-border transactions, including the direct exchange markets, and to support the development of yen- and RMB-based bond markets as well as yen- and RMB-denominated financial products. As a result of this agreement, Japan became the first country besides the United States to engage in direct RMB currency exchange with China. But the overall amount of direct currency trading between the two countries has thus far been limited.

A quarterly branch meeting at the Bank of Japan's headquarters in Tokyo, April 2016.

JAPAN'S ENGAGEMENT WITH THE RMB

Five years after the initial burst of cooperation, on December 22, 2017, the monetary authorities of Japan and China finally approved allowing Japanese corporations to issue RMB-based bonds (so-called "Panda bonds") in China. Nonetheless, the Japanese government has still not signed on to any of the four important initiatives that the Chinese government has advanced to promote RMB internationalization. The first was the bilateral currency swap arrangement that the Chinese monetary authority extended to more than 30 countries around the world after the global financial crisis. Although the Japanese government was the first to conduct a currency swap with China under the CMI, it has not renewed the arrangement since it expired in September 2013.

Second, Japan has yet to acquire RMB Qualified Foreign Institutional Investor (RQFII) status, which would allow Japanese institutions to invest in RMB-based assets in China. As of January 2017, institutional investors from 16 countries besides Hong Kong and Taiwan are registered, totaling RMB 529.6 billion (US$77.2 billion) worth of quota.

The third initiative is related to the RMB payment settlement system. In 2014, China's offshore financial centers expanded beyond Hong Kong, Taiwan, and Singapore when China's central bank established deals with banks in several countries, including Australia, Canada, Germany, Malaysia, Thailand, and the United Kingdom.

The memoranda of understanding afforded these banks direct access to China's National Advanced Payment System, which functions as an electronic inter-bank clearing and settlement system. Furthermore, to compete against the payment clearing and settlement service offered globally by SWIFT, China launched in October 2015 the Cross-Border Inter-Bank Payment System (also called the China International Payment System; CIPS), through which foreign banks can access RMB settlement directly. In both cases, no Japanese banks participated, restricting Tokyo's role in the RMB business.

Finally, the Japanese government has thus far stayed out of the Asian Infrastructure Investment Bank (AIIB), which Chinese President Xi Jinping proposed in October 2013 and came into existence in January 2016 with a $100 billion funding base. Though it is still unclear how much of the AIIB's future projects will be denominated in RMB, many suspect that the establishment of the AIIB and China's concurrent "Belt and Road Initiative" would contribute to RMB internationalization by expanding RMB-denominated investment in the region.

Japan's refusal to join the AIIB came in spite of heavy courting by the Chinese leadership, as China hoped to increase the institution's legitimacy in Asia. Japanese hesitancy might relate to the fact that China has been dragging its feet on RQFII approval for Japan and the installment of an RMB clearing bank in Tokyo.

Now that the easy part of RMB internationalization—trade settlement—has been achieved, the rest of the process will depend on market forces and the Chinese authority's will and ability to liberalize its domestic financial markets. Of course, China's slowing economic growth adds to such concern. It took Japan more than 20 years to go through this process, and even that was not enough to urge market players to follow. Given the multiple economic and political difficulties Japan has experienced in the process, Japanese experts and officials are not holding their collective breath that China can achieve such feats anytime soon.

Japan, the second-largest economy in Asia with a sophisticated financial sector and experience in financial liberalization, has been slow to ride on the RMB internationalization wave.

EASIER SAID THAN DONE

Japan, the second-largest economy in Asia with a sophisticated financial sector and experience in financial liberalization, has been slow to ride on the RMB internationalization wave. In turn, Japan has contributed to the dollar's persistent dominance in Asia. At the same time, the Japanese economy is becoming sensitive to currency competition as the country deepens its financial integration with the rest of the world.

Since December 2012, Abenomics, named after sitting Prime Minister Shinzo Abe, has become Japan's main economic growth strategy. The first of three arrows of this strategy, an aggressive monetary easing policy (conducted by Bank of Japan Governor Haruhiko Kuroda since April 2013), led to a quick depreciation of the yen against the dollar. The resulted in both economic growth and accusations of currency manipulation. With the U.S. Federal Reserve recently beginning to take steps to raise the country's discount rate under the strengthening dollar, the currency conflict is bound to intensify.

Meanwhile, a cheaper yen and booming stock market have invited further inward foreign investment in Japan, which also includes an increased proportion of foreign ownership in the Japanese government's short-term debt (Treasury Bills and Financial Bills, whose maturity is less than one year) from 28.6 percent in March 2013 to 50.9 percent in December 2016. Some report that the bulk of such foreign ownership comes from China, whose monetary authority has worked to diversify the composition of its still-massive foreign exchange reserves.

A stable currency environment is the key component that has underpinned Asia's economic success in the post-1945 period, for Japan between the 1950s and the early 1970s and for China from the 1980s to recently. It was the U.S. dollar that provided such an environment. Because of that, the Japanese government has been an unequivocal supporter of dollar dominance. Now, China faces the dilemma it saw in Japan's yen internationalization experience: prioritize stability in both the regional currency environment and domestic financial conditions and lose the golden opportunity to alter the regional currency hierarchy. The Japanese experience shows that there is not much time left for Chinese leaders to make the final decision.

SAORI N. KATADA is Associate Professor of International Relations at the University of Southern California.

China and the International Monetary System

Does Beijing Really Want to Challenge the Dollar?

Hongying Wang

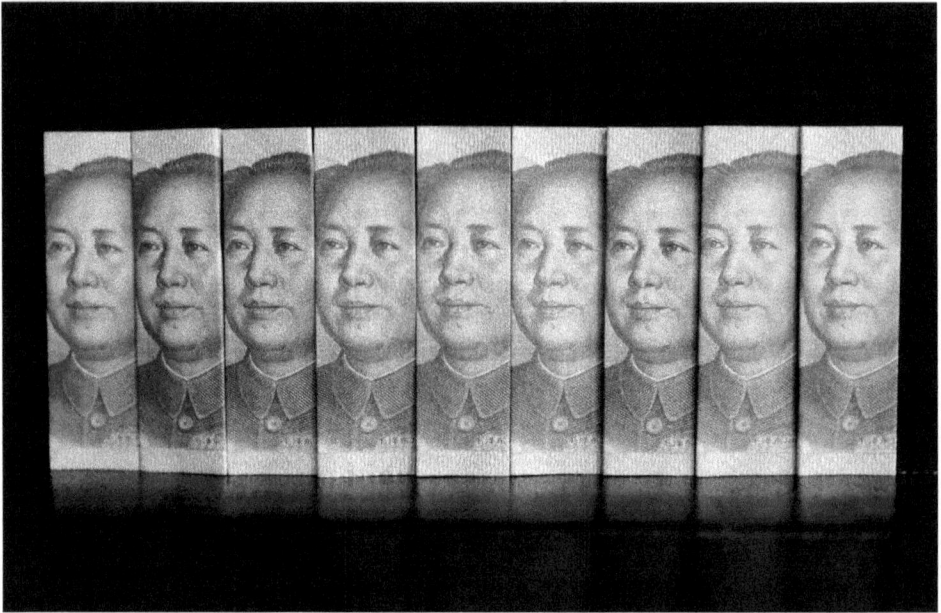

Chinese banknotes in Beijing, July 2011.

In March 2009, a few months after the outbreak of the global financial crisis, the governor of China's central bank, Zhou Xiaochuan, published an essay on the bank's website. Zhou criticized the international monetary system for "the inherent deficiencies caused by using credit-based national currencies" and praised the Special Drawing Right (SDR), the synthetic currency created by the International Monetary Fund (IMF). The SDR "serves as the light in the tunnel for the reform of the international monetary system," Zhou wrote.

Zhou's call for a greater role for the SDR attracted attention around the world. Many observers viewed his comments as a sign of China's readiness to challenge the U.S.-dominated international monetary order. Indeed, several years later, in 2015, China got its own currency, the renminbi (RMB), admitted to the SDR basket, which the year before had included only the dollar, the pound sterling, the yen, and the euro. Some Western analysts saw that measure, too, as a sign of China's interest in challenging the international monetary system.

In fact, Zhou's 2009 statement was not as revolutionary as it seemed. His comments reflected China's long-standing position that the SDR should play a greater role in the international monetary system, making it less detrimental to developing countries and easing some of the instability produced by its dependence on national currencies as reserves. That position says more about China's national identity than about its interest in challenging the U.S.-dominated international monetary system.

IMF Managing Director Christine Lagarde and Chinese President Xi Jinping in Boao, China, April 2013.

THE EMERGENCE OF THE SDR

The international monetary system created at the end of World War II was based on fixed exchange rates and a strong link between the dollar and gold. By the early 1960s, the economist Robert Triffin had identified a major weakness in this system: the country that issued the global reserve currency (in this case, the United States) had to supply the world with liquidity in its currency—but to do so, it had to run balance-of-payments deficits, which would erode the world's confidence in the currency. Over the course of the decade, the so-called Triffin dilemma became a widely recognized reality. In 1969, to address the problem, the IMF created the SDR to supplement the U.S. dollar as a source of international liquidity; in 1970, it made its first allocation of

SDR 9.3 billion. (The value of the SDR fluctuates with the value of the currencies on which it is based.)

The new synthetic currency was a marginal factor in the international monetary system—and it became only more so over time. Indeed, from the 1970s to the 1990s, the share of SDRs in global nongold reserves declined from nine percent to between one and two percent. By the early years of this century, the SDR seemed mostly irrelevant.

That trend underwent a dramatic reversal in the aftermath of the global financial crisis. Many observers, such as the political economist Eric Helleiner, credited Zhou's comments for the revived interest. But did Zhou's views really represent a radical break from China's earlier approach to the reform of the global monetary system? History suggests otherwise.

CHINA JOINS THE CLUB

By the time the People's Republic of China joined the IMF in 1980, the original Bretton Woods system had gone through tumultuous changes. The United States had broken the link between gold and the U.S. dollar in 1971, rendering moot the original purpose of the SDR—that is, to supplement the dollar under a fixed exchange rate. In 1978, the IMF set forth the objective of making the SDR a principal reserve currency; the next year, it made a second allocation of about SDR 12 billion.

In its first years as a member of the IMF and the World Bank, Beijing showed itself to be a modest, cooperative newcomer. When it came to the SDR, China tended to rely on reports and studies issued by the IMF's staff, largely agreeing with their recommendations. But over the years that followed, Beijing began to lobby for the allocation of more SDRs, a more equitable distribution of the synthetic currency, and an expanded use of the SDR more generally.

Why did China push for these policies? In the early 1980s, Chinese representatives at the IMF contended that Western official development assistance was not meeting the growing financing needs of most poorer countries. China argued that more SDR allocations could reduce those countries' need to borrow abroad, help them expand their imports, and let their economies grow. Around a decade later, in a 1992 speech at the IMF, China's representative to the organization, Che Peiqin, made a similar case. Che argued that countries in sub-Saharan Africa and eastern Europe had seen a considerable decline in the ratio of nongold reserves to imports. Without easy access to the international capital markets, they struggled to restore their reserve ratios, at the expense of imports and growth. It would be in the interest of all, Che argued, to make more official resources available to those states.

After the Asian financial crisis of 1997–98, foreign direct investment in developing economies was slowing, the balance of payments among many poorer countries was taking a hit, and such countries were facing high costs to borrow in international markets. So China again called for more SDR allocations. Increasing the allocation of SDRs, Beijing argued, would help stabilize the international financial system by providing a safeguard against liquidity crises among developing countries.

The distribution of SDRs was another focus of Chinese policy. According to the IMF's Articles of Agreement, new allocations of SDRs would be distributed according to members' IMF quotas, meaning that developed countries, which hold the biggest quotas, would get more SDRs than would developing countries. China took issue with this distribution, and on several occasions, Beijing's representatives to the IMF called for the organization to redistribute some of the SDRs so that they would benefit developing countries.

The first two drivers of China's interest in SDRs—liquidity and distribution—thus took preference over what today's observers regard as the core of Chinese policy: expanding the role of the SDR in the international monetary system.

Yet that third theme was present as far back as 1986. In a speech at the IMF in that year, China's representative, Huang Fanzhang, argued that because creditworthy countries (generally developed ones) could augment their reserves by borrowing in the market without having to undertake specific adjustment measures, they could delay correcting the imbalances that had led to the borrowing until they had reached a point where they had to take tough measures. Huang also pointed out that financial markets tend to overreact, oscillating between overlending and panicking. That meant that the SDR held great potential to improve the management of international liquidity: by increasing the share of the SDR in international reserves, the reserve-generating process would become less volatile, since it would be less dependent on private capital markets.

In 1989, China's representative to the IMF, Dai Qianding, called on the agency to broaden the use of the SDR by permitting private entities to employ it and by simplifying the processes by which it could be used. In the long term, Dai told the IMF, "there is no firm assurance in relying on a national currency as an international reserve asset," so it was appropriate to explore making the SDR the international monetary system's principal reserve asset. In 1994, Wei Benhua, the Chinese representative at the IMF, went further. "We must make efforts in moving toward the objective of making the SDR the principal reserve asset of the international monetary system," he said.

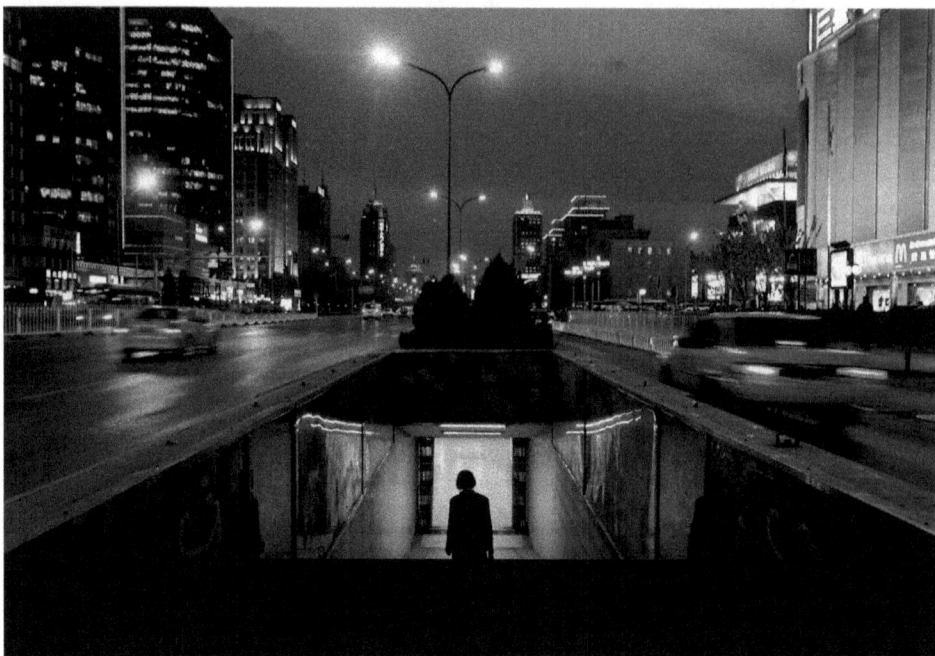

In Beijing's central business district, April 2007.

CHALLENGING WHAT'S IN THE BASKET

Since 1980, the SDR basket had included the currencies of the five IMF members with the largest exports of goods and services between 1975 and 1979: the U.S. dollar, German mark, French franc, Japanese yen, and British pound sterling. (The mark and the franc were replaced by the euro after the introduction of that currency.) In the 1980s and 1990s, China went along with the method and basket used by the IMF to decide the value and the interest rate of the SDR.

But China's position began to change in the years that followed. In 2005, a statement China submitted to the IMF criticized the IMF for using "backward-looking indicators" in developing the SDR basket and suggested that the institution discuss China's rapid growth as an exporter. The implication was clear: the IMF should consider the RMB for inclusion in the SDR basket. By 2009, after Zhou's statement, Chinese representatives at the IMF again argued that in order to improve the liquidity and attractiveness of the SDR as a reserve asset, IMF staff should study how to broaden the role of the SDR, expanding and realigning the currencies in the SDR basket.

In 2010, in a review of the SDR basket, the IMF rejected the RMB's attempt to enter. But China did not give up. At the G-20 summit in St. Petersburg in 2013, Chinese President Xi Jinping again called on the IMF to reform the SDR basket, and in 2015 the Chinese government intensified its push. Finally, in November 2015, the IMF decided to accept the RMB into the SDR basket, assigning it 10.92 percent of the total weight, below the U.S. dollar and the euro, but above the yen and the pound sterling.

CURRENCY POLITICS IN CONTEXT

Contrary to widely held impressions, then, Zhou's 2009 statement was not a major departure from China's longstanding positions regarding the SDR or the dollar-led order. Instead, it represented a reprisal of ideas that Beijing had pushed for decades: namely, that the international monetary system was burdened by its dependence on private capital markets and a few national currencies, the dollar chief among them.

What was notable about Zhou's statement was not its content but its timing. In the late 1990s, when the IMF decided to allocate more SDRs for the first time since the early 1980s, China's economy was the world's seventh largest, ranking behind Italy's. By 2009, however, China's GDP had become the third largest in the world, after the United States' and Japan's. More important, the global financial crisis, which originated in the United States, had dealt a heavy blow to the prestige of many developed countries: China stood almost alone as the world's remaining major engine of growth. So when Zhou had something to say about reforming the international monetary system, the world listened—even though Chinese representatives had been saying similar things for quite a while and even though others, such as a commission of economists led by the American Joseph Stiglitz, were making similar proposals about the SDR.

Yuri Gripas / REUTERS

At the headquarters of the International Monetary Fund in Washington, October 2014.

NATIONAL IDENTITY AND CHINA'S SDR POLICY

China's long-standing support for the SDR can't be neatly explained in terms of its economic interests. For years, the Chinese government advocated new SDR allocations and a more equitable SDR distribution, arguing that those changes would help developing countries deal with their balance-of-payments problems. From the early 1980s to the early 1990s, when China had limited export capacity and was itself a developing country, this position could have benefited China. But since the early 1990s, China has been a massive exporter, with a current account surplus to match. Its support for the expansion of the SDR thus seems to have diverged from its own economic interests. It is also unclear how China's economic goals are being served by Beijing's calls to make the SDR a more reliable and stable source of international liquidity, thereby eventually making it the world's principal reserve asset. In fact, there is good reason for Beijing to eschew a bigger role for the SDR. A more important SDR would spell a decline in the dollar's role and value, and that would cost China, which is a major holder of dollar assets.

Nor is this all. In order for the RMB to enter the SDR basket, it would need to meet the IMF's standards of being "widely used" and "freely usable." China had to take some big steps toward financial liberalization to get it there. Some analysts cautioned that these radical adjustments would bring considerable risks to China's financial system. Others pointed out that the RMB's inclusion in the SDR basket would neither turn the RMB into a major reserve currency nor make the SDR a substitute for the U.S. dollar.

After Beijing began to push for the RMB's entry into the SDR basket in the first decade of this century, the prevailing opinion in China remained cautious. Although some argued that the SDR would gain more relevance once it included China's currency, many commentators continued to point out the SDR's limitations, and influential observers, such as the former central bank governor Dai Xianglong, predicted that the future of the international monetary system would involve a number of national currencies rather than a suprasovereign one such as the SDR.

If Beijing's SDR policy seems inexplicable in light of the country's material interests, it makes a good deal of sense when China's national identity is taken into account. When Beijing joined the IMF in 1980, it identified as a member of the developing world, and it stuck to that identity in international forums. Indeed, according to research by the political scientists Harold Karan Jacobson and Michel Oksenberg, Chinese officials at both the World Bank and the IMF were under instructions from Beijing not to raise demands that might be seen as costly to any developing country. Supporting the SDR as a tool of economic development went hand in hand with China's identification with the global South.

Since the late 1990s, another identity has gradually taken hold in the Chinese imagination: that of a major power. Beijing's performance during the Asian financial crisis played a big part. As its neighboring countries' currencies took a dive in 1997 and 1998, China faced tremendous pressure to devalue the RMB. It refused to do so, and although Chinese exports suffered heavily, Beijing drew praise from around the world, affirming its self-perception as a "responsible great power." Then came the years after 2007, when China hosted the Olympics, sent its first astronauts to walk in space, and preserved the growth of its economy as the United States fell into its worst financial crisis in decades. Joining the SDR basket may have involved financial risks, but it also promised an intangible reward in the form of international prestige. In late 2015, when the IMF finally approved the Chinese currency's entry into the SDR basket, it was warmly celebrated in China. For China's leaders and for the Chinese public, the news was a clear sign of China's rising international status.

China's advocacy of a greater role for the SDR in the international monetary system since the global financial crisis, then, has not been as revolutionary as it seems. Nor is it necessarily meant to challenge the dollar-dominated order. Beijing's SDR policy has been more about affirming China's national identity than about advancing its material interests.

HONGYING WANG is Associate Professor of Political Science at the University of Waterloo and a Senior Fellow at the Centre for International Governance Innovation in Canada.

www.ingramcontent.com/pod-product-compliance
Lightning Source LLC
Chambersburg PA
CBHW050241290326
41930CB00043B/3294